AF270627

Bernese Mountain Dogs

by Julie Murray

abdobooks.com

Published by Abdo Kids, a division of ABDO, P.O. Box 398166, Minneapolis, Minnesota 55439.
Copyright © 2024 by Abdo Consulting Group, Inc. International copyrights reserved in all countries.
No part of this book may be reproduced in any form without written permission from the publisher.
Abdo Kids Jumbo™ is a trademark and logo of Abdo Kids.

Printed in the United States of America, North Mankato, Minnesota.

102023

012024

THIS BOOK CONTAINS
RECYCLED MATERIALS

Photo Credits: Alamy, Getty Images, Shutterstock, Thinkstock

Production Contributors: Teddy Borth, Jennie Forsberg, Grace Hansen
Design Contributors: Candice Keimig, Pakou Moua

Library of Congress Control Number: 2023937685
Publisher's Cataloging-in-Publication Data

Names: Murray, Julie, author.

Title: Bernese mountain dogs / by Julie Murray

Description: Minneapolis, Minnesota : Abdo Kids, 2024 | Series: Dogs | Includes online resources and
    index.

Identifiers: ISBN 9781098268503 (lib. bdg.) | ISBN 9781098269203 (ebook) | ISBN 9781098269555
    (Read-to-Me ebook)

Subjects: LCSH: Bernese mountain dog--Juvenile literature. | Working dogs--Juvenile literature. | Dogs--
    Juvenile literature. | Dogs--Behavior--Juvenile literature. | Animal behavior--Juvenile literature.

Classification: DDC 599.772--dc23

Table of Contents

Bernese Mountain Dogs

Bernese mountain dogs are often called Berners. They are large dogs with big hearts.

Berners **originated** in the farmlands of Switzerland more than 2,000 years ago. They were **bred** to herd **livestock** and haul heavy loads.

Europe
Switzerland
N
W E
S

Berners have strong, muscular bodies. They can stand up to 27 inches (68.6 cm) tall. They weigh up to 115 pounds (52 kg)!

Berners have black, white, and **rust** colored coats. The coat is medium in length. It is thick and made up of two layers. It can be straight or wavy.

Grooming

Berners shed a lot! They need to be brushed often. This will keep their coats healthy and tangle-free.

13

Exercise

Berners need daily exercise.
Large, fenced yards are best
for them to safely run and play.
Long walks are good too!

Berners are made for the cold.
They love outdoor activities
such as hiking and playing
in the snow. They can easily
overheat, so they should not
be overworked on hot days.

Personality

Berners are very smart and easy to train. They make great family pets. They also get along with other animals.

Berners are gentle giants. They
are known for being loving and
loyal toward their families.

More Facts

- Bernese mountain dogs are named for the state of Bern in Switzerland. This is in the Bernese Alps.

- Berners can have serious health issues. Because of this, their lifespan is just 6 to 10 years. Using responsible **breeders** is important.

- Berners first came to the United States in 1926. The American Kennel Club officially recognized the breed in 1937.

Glossary

bred – developed over time for a certain purpose.

breeder – one whose job is to breed animals.

livestock – cows, horses, sheep, or other animals raised or kept on a farm or ranch.

loyal – showing devotion and faithfulness to someone.

originated – came from or began in a particular place or situation.

rust – reddish-brown or reddish-yellow in color.

23

Index

body 8

coat 10, 12

colors 10

exercise 14, 16

grooming 12

history 6

personality 4, 16, 18, 20

size 4, 8, 20

Switzerland 6

training 18

Visit **abdokids.com** to access crafts, games, videos, and more!